BLOOD BODY

LAUREN CROWLEY

Also by Lauren Crowley

BAPTISM

Copyright © 2017 by Lauren Crowley

All rights reserved. No part of this book may be used or reproduced in any manner whatsoever without written permission except in the case of brief quotations embodied in critical articles and reviews.

First paperback edition published in 2017 by Crowley Press
CrowleyPress.com

Printed in the United States of America

Library of Congress Cataloging-in-Publication Data
ISBN: 978-0-9982322-1-8
1. Poetry 2. Witchcraft

to Drew

Contents

Part I / 1
Part II / 36
Part III / 63
Part IV / 84
Part V / 118
Part VI / 148

Part I

CROWLEY

we have the same bones
and when I lie next to you I have none
I rest my head on your shoulder and breathe life's air
dumbly, an ingenue. we found life's formula, a return to the garden.
fleshly, and knowing, too.

-October 7, 2016

BLOOD BODY

and the maenad's rise from the turquoise swamp,
the lake, the moss, their fingers, won't stop,
and we hear them, from the place of our home,
their burning, the dissolving, of what we are not,
and curses, throw the rock, into the lake of our
remembrance, think me not, a solemn soul full of
wishes but

the creator
of god's earlier thought

CROWLEY

through - and through - and through
pulled by the arms, knees in the mud
of our amniotic fluid, a songstress leads
as eyes tremble with delight. the path,
our wood, and the shadows that cure
take the one key, you know what to do

do we hear him, his flute,
as we fall into sleep,
and become only roots

-October 9, 2016

BLOOD BODY

a satanic witch - a sorcerous witch
a setting of cold fire and red-riddled reed
a surly witch - a scorpio witch
a settling into that cold, wet fire

who feeds you? but the dark one,
the darkened night, our
darkened room

who strains you? but the
eyes that cannot see,
and their words,
and how they think of thee,

but the
black hair in the water,
and the moonlit raw
oh how she greets me
when i become small

devourous, undeeming,
deliverance, beseeching

(put my hands in your mouth
so you may taste me
we are the only ones
worth saving)

We are-
decaying,
fleshless,
unsavory

selecting and enchanting,
selecting and enchanting,
we are
purposefully planning,
digging up and planting

marionettes ever dancing
allowing, entrancing

see as our feet make their way
and for the first time, we are
standing

beneath our bones,
decanting
decanting

BLOOD BODY

in the teeth grove we hide,
as the gods march on by
collecting and smelling
the fear in our lungs

is the flesh torn apart?
when their eyes seem to wander
and we couldn't be wronger -
they do like to bite

and to ravish,
I saw my red satin dress
fall to the floor

the rapture,
our capture,
is pagan
once more

CROWLEY

you found
the red room in my
skin, the door, ajar
our hands, untaught
my limbs like four
snakes, and I, the
red-moon queen,
felt without thought

BLOOD BODY

to enjoy a reddened fruit -
and to be the one most willing
a woman, offending

to walk down dark halls
and find yourself
splaying

to inhabit a body

the woman
at the beach

and the girl
who dreamed of being

(stolen, taken,
the face on
milk cartons)

CROWLEY

and there is a starlit chapel,
where I lay myself on the table
an offering, made fae or fable,
the woman of the vines, and her
star-crossed tale

the salvation of god's tender light
our mother's dark hands, the night
the night

each inch of skin, a line from
the modern-day bible

                              -October 11, 2016

BLOOD BODY

we are
a locked box,
looking for
pandora

-October 12, 2016

CROWLEY

and to sing the midnight dirge,

we are always burying, burying
skins we thought were ours, no,
they were illusions, happenstance
contusions, no, we needn't be the
body ripped in two. a monster we've
become, a monster we'll undo

BLOOD BODY

bell-bottomed genie, aquarian baby, we left the cult and became our beginning, in a dream they quoted me but erased the devil's name, I sing in blood-red they mistake it as pain. as if I'm stitching the words into skin and not humming them in heaven, the woman in the convent writhing and warbling.
and relaxing, as she sinks to the floor. the signature below her center, we adore, we adore. and I woke up amorous, as the ravens opened my box. peeled back the skin, ate up the rot. falling asleep into shades of red, by the blood we awaken by the blood we are fed.

CROWLEY

I whispered my words into the chilled and dark mirror,
the fog of my breath makes the image seem clearer
and I pronounce myself whole, a spirited seer,
a mother of ghosts, beckon them nearer

oh sacred and sloven,
our wistful heart cloven,
our love and this home,
the door in this poem

BLOOD BODY

And She Rose

her fleshed form from the cemetery floor
the grey hill and how it held her
pristine and pale, her dark and dim tale
and how the light was born, a candle's flame
that spoke to her smoothly, restore me, in your
soul. cast away their chains, and let your sinews
simmer, salute thee, we do, as our glow grows
dimmer, and you snarl and whimper, girl, girl,
sinner

(we are of the leaves, one with the thieves, who knew the light could be seen better from the earth's dark interior)

CROWLEY

from her casket she does not see
the red roses, the river of blood
and the air, how it holds a musk,
dark and new

the current of her belonging,
and the promise of renewal,

a woman for a warrior
armourless, Amorous
aiming too soon

from the battlefield I saw you
and you saw me, too

-October 13, 2016

BLOOD BODY

the fence and our burning it down. i set the match and waited, made sure nothing survived.

the fence and our turning around. I did not look at it, I merely walked on by.

it does not exist. it does not exist.
it does not dictate.

I walked by the fence and saw only wood

-October 14, 2016

CROWLEY

emergence, resurgence,
the woman above water

her toes do not touch,
faith does not falter

the oracle, her incense
wafting and Knowing

the priests and their bells,
ringing, extolling,

smoke covers our eyes,
we're blind or we're open

beholden,
are we chosen?
no,
no, stolen

by the gospel of our devotion

BLOOD BODY

I am a drinker of
The Precious Blood

carry me down the concrete steps
beast, in the night, the ivory moonlight,
we are forsaken

for resembling the snake,
and coveting the earth
for lips,
rose-hips,

we do not awaken when
we find ourselves taken
sub rosa,

under his moon

CROWLEY

autumn clutches me with her claws,
until I, too, dissolve into leaves,
in the forest, you know this,
we were born to be dreams

red robin, I saw you, and
forgot to be real, the bones
crack, and I gasp, the heart
made a deal

and the girl of cool water,
her eyes of the trees,
her dew-crystal wings,
natural things

the honey-lit cabin,
made of warm wood
the light of your mind
left me understood

but a child, but a shrew
you, you, we're two

trees changing leaves
on the same hallowed eve

BLOOD BODY

a small box, tucked away, this is where the love stays
would i open it, there would only be empty, and
in your hands, the phantoms of words

living, breathing, gold-encrusted beings,
singeing the hairs on your arms,

i sit in the underworld, while they find you above

surely, you already saw
the gold flakes in my eyes
how they hymn and they call

how four days in, the valley
was flooded in fragrant light,
nature knew us, and to us it
was kind

CROWLEY

above and below,
the wind seems to blow,
through invisible holes
unseen and unknown

inside, a place of forgotten,
a place of just being,
together, softly
no roles,

only your hands, to hold
(and the heart seems to dance,
when we're young, when we're old)

-October 16, 2016

BLOOD BODY

and now, in October,
there is only my willowy frame
and the Flame of the Blood

the dragon's mark and
the womanly flood

as you lay me down in
the shadowy wood,

I keep to you
I kiss you,

I am only good

(the way he wove my black velvet hood,
in stitches, blood of witches, serpentine sainthood)

CROWLEY

the grain blowing slowly,
"the trees are always dancing, we just don't see it"
I'm sitting on a round stone, with the ether's dripping soul
surrounding, and it seems there is a space between,
sincerely, I lay my cards on woodwick tables,
surrendering,

I promised you this.
full bloom, imbued
life in the dew

flames,

BLOOD BODY

when the gods sleep,
and they dream about me
am I sitting on thrones of
skull, rot, and thistle?

or lying in bed,
pink halo round my head
breathing the wings of
angel food cake and
communion bread

am I counting the hours
until God grants me showers
of unity fruit,
capsized we're drowning,
too

(i love, i love you
they hear my heart brimming
with caramel goo)

-October 17, 2016

CROWLEY

written on the back of her hand
I want to be Possessed

if the thorns around her neck dig deeper
Will she feel it?

if she found her body buried in a ditch
would she rest,

would we rather be a pile of flesh
or the ghost, unseen, unfelt

we'd rather be undressed

BLOOD BODY

the woman on the leather couch,
upward eyes and a loosening mouth

what comes out -
but the eighth plague,
the lacuna's filled with locusts
and the confessor hasn't much to say

I seized on the labyrinth
and burnt it down,
the hotel in the mountains
is quiet today

falling, falling away
stitched to my lips
the devil's debt to pay

in the inferno we
have a dream of
that firefly,
v u l n e r a b i l i t y

-October 18, 2016

CROWLEY

from the womb my red pours out, the hot blood,
white heat, white noise, I am caught by the satyrs,
they hold me, I hold myself, in my room, the flood
it's all too much, just enough, so sweet, the feeling
the burnt orange of leaves, the eyes in the shadows
these are our offerings, haunt and heat

the veins are wide highways, and I'm gushing
a woman of Babalon, the Scarlet Woman
the rose has overgrown
and it bleeds out

and we lap it from the floor,
until the light goes out

vampire woman, found her own fountain

-October 19, 2016

BLOOD BODY

if i could be wrapped in the stardust all the time,
if my eyes were nothing but that light,
our limbs would move as the willow does,
our mouth hanging open, like a sleeping child

and if the trees always held my hand,
i would not wander off into the graveyard

just fill my head with it
morning's light
and holy water

the giant gods in the ocean led me to you

in the night they loom above me,
I shrink until there's only room for
the things that are true

BLOOD BODY

the woman of Pan and her
fateful signature, caressed by the
blood-ink that drips from her fingers

and mingles - her oils into clay,
pronounced by the day
she bursts through the page

and she takes, and she takes
the fallen debris, plucking the weeds
until purity's me,

newness, I'll do this,
gazing, wondering,
free

-October 21, 2016

fullness, no other word lands on our windowsill,
just, imagine - each cell, warm with the orange glow
each word, fateful, pieces of a prayer. perfect, the
word we do not know, an apple before us, but
could it be spoken by the heart, as all things should be
fullness, fuller, fallen, we fainted into sleep, a thousand
dreams, spoke to us, singing, fuller, fullness
fortune, kissed us

and we kissed back, through the fetters we
held the body of providence

BLOOD BODY

capricorn's icy fingers and
his forgotten horns,
we only swim beneath
when there's a storm,

and in the gardens,
we become much more,
do you see, how he breathes deep,
when he is alone

and he is the devil's favorite,
how they play and they mourn

CROWLEY

we stood at the rim of the volcano,
hidden in the mountains, on a
still black night
and as the fire rushed before us
and turned our body yellow,
we became god's light

we were the
angel of the earth
and the devil of the sky,
what fell from the heavens
awoke here tonight

and we were its ruler
the fallen creator-
the magick indweller-
the source and the light

i saw you surrender
somnambulant,
without a fight

                                                            -October 22, 2016

BLOOD BODY

i fell asleep in the folds of my body, in smooth flesh,
a honeycomb, the home i had forgotten

womanhood without initiation, i awoke in a waterfall
and the song that they were playing
didn't displease at all

-October 24, 2016

Part II

BLOOD BODY

the way we find ourselves drifting closer to the black sky,
that is how i want to be

gravity pulls to my heart that which
we desire

i am fuller, fullest
marinated in magickal codes

receptivity, i receive ye
fuller, fullest

the canyon and the night

the coyote sleeping alone,
no fears, no home

CROWLEY

i only feel my body through words-
through the poetry that feeds me,
a child eating quickly

though I know the trees,
and the way they know me

though we are a butterfly
flying off, capitulating

and I beg you to capture me
between two hips, two wings

sour things, bite to please,
promises weave, oh I see

softly, harder, fuller
fullest

faun in the night
my body is a myth
I heard only once

BLOOD BODY

secluded to her home
the maiden cracked the alchemist's code
and now she's pouring out gold
from her well-worn heart, young but old

and it floods the floors
the divine child asks for more

eros, sucking and kissing at
the universe's hands

CROWLEY

some new thought
cocks their head
to a door unnoticed,
takes the keys,
and unlocks it

and there is the wedding altar,
and the stars

BLOOD BODY

when my hair touches the ground we'll say
we've left heaven
and found a chthonic tonic for our
shaky limbs

and we'll stand in the mirror and
try to convince ourselves we
know what we see,

we'll drape costumes over our frame
stories we haven't found the words for,
not yet

i am a
woman who creates herself

one who
hears the whispering inside of the marble

marvel, at what we choose to be

-October 25, 2016

like i had opened the door and let it all out,
no one in, full of doubt. and we surrounded
with roses and we talked to the moon, but
something was missing and my heart had
grown blue, beating but bruised, the only
evidence of blood

and your kisses, against the sheet i was
wrapped in, woke up a ghost and who
forgot how to swim, and i say what are
these legs for if not giving in, what are
these hands for but lighthearted sin,

am i a
woman or an image
printed onto a page,

i saw in the mirror
the flesh that could save

and i prayed it away
the doubt and the rage

full of the soul stream
that awaited this day

(destiny, destiny. fate fate fate)

-October 26, 2016

BLOOD BODY

I want to give you
lavender and bruised flesh,
I want to give you
the kitten inside,

the rings on my fingers and
the source of my soul,

the blue land and our blossoming,
here on earth, destiny, fate, focus

i was
dreaming of you

and the lyre played
until the heart grew out

-October 28, 2016

CROWLEY

watch me, us, step into the golden feet of
merciless magick and teaseful delight,
i'm
foolishly planning a lovesacred night,
we walked through dark shadows to find
only light,

we're human. we'll do this
our one and only rite

BLOOD BODY

fallen before us we will not ignore this the way our lips smatter secrets and kissing is endless and i found the door in my tongue and the way it could tell this, the blushing soft flesh and the distant dark places. could you call me back? or are my hands tied in mud I saw the keys sinking lower and I had to go further and you asked me what's wrong, nothing at all. except my eyes are too blue and the brown of yours is thicker and I can't hardly remember what took me that far. I'll kiss it away I'm an angel today, my heart will grow fonder and we will not wonder like the sun has been setting on oceans of blessing and we will swim on, a heart and a wand

you sang me my song

(you were here all along)

-October 29, 2016

CROWLEY

There is a black manor in which I've lived,
a leg or an arm, dismembered by time gone by,
during the new moon we remembered, descended
aligned

the father in the fortress, and his musical ways
horned or hoofed, with skin like mine

every time we pledged on our knees we
were reaching for our own tarred souls

tumultuous, endings, beginning, again

maybe rhyming is hard when you're running through the leaves,
the river we're complete, the sorcerer and his feat, grabbing the
winged-screech

no words, just ease

-October 30, 2016

BLOOD BODY

the berried room, the burning remembering,
I buried you in
sugar, you came to me, cleansing

the gifts of the fall,
encircling, surrendering

slithering,
the heart and the womb

ensorcelling,
released from my tomb

I kissed you-
we kissed until blue

(made of water, made of food)

a song played on loop -
I fall, I fall in love with you

CROWLEY

sleepy baby,
red-footed maybe,
a star in our eyes,
I took to you lately

encase me, I'll cross my arms across my chest and sing our song, pink wisp of smoke will leave my lips as I grow gone, into the earth with the spirits that roam, they smile for me safely and the trees laughed like crazy, and I could laugh, too, the woman, so new

the heart is a velvet divan, red lit blue, by the so-loving moon, sewn by an angel or two, for us to sit on.

and I spread out - there is space for my surrender, for rose tea, chocolate, you

-October 31, 2016

BLOOD BODY

I was born a woman -
full-blooded and demon-tailed
like my spirit had left my body,
sitting next to me, next to blonde-
haired legs, next to black nails,
next to my corpse, hearing my wails

heeding my cries, she stayed at my side
unsure of what to say

crawling in my bed at night,
filling me up, until I filled her
embodiment. embalming fluid

my wings become real

                                                                  -November 1, 2016

CROWLEY

my arms push against tough cocoon walls - may we come out? may we play? may we make some food today? may we roll around in the light of day, as hair shines oils and hips will sway - I say, the devil's in my pantry eating marshmallow cream, and I'm tending the furnace, it's not what it seems

we laid below the Sun and had our good pleasure, the skin of my arms couldn't be any thinner, and so when we fall on our knees are we saint or are we sinner, god kisses me at night and he ate me for dinner.

I fell to my knees, I fell to my knees, prayed that no one would see, the harlot in me

BLOOD BODY

poetry as apotheosis

as I rattled my chains, and thought about my jail
as I breathed the universe in and breathed me out
as I gasped for air, choking on a false duality
as I traveled through time

as I got on all fours and sunk my hands into black earth
as I burnt it all down

as I painted a paradise

poetry as apotheosis

the only thing that could contain this

how many hours do we spend hiding the flesh -
as if to be seen means to be burnt,

HERETIC on the witch's pyre
hardly there, remember how we floated upon death
a lucid dream, and "I was right"

how she writhed and convulsed...
and how she liked it, divine communion,
priestess of the fire

and the Sun-
don't you see,
how the Holy Father commends,
how he's been waiting to be
touched, embraced, saved

(the rooms of heaven are in each molecule of air)

BLOOD BODY

the devil stole me from my cradle
and cradled my bones,
he said Their lashes will hurt you
in a place that you can't find, and
you'll spend a lifetime building upon
it, until that which you create is
the only thing that can be seen

-November 2, 2016

CROWLEY

you can't write a poem about a war
but you can point to the spilled blood,
sinking into the soil

and if every woman bottled her rage
and sold it for bread,

she would never go hungry
she would always be fed

and if I whispered of mine
I would be out of line

so I write about bread
and spill blood instead

(there's a war in my head and I am not winning it, but I will)

-November 3, 2016

BLOOD BODY

this is the nocturne of the body
some things it only says in the dark-
and we wrestle them out, cold white
doubt, feeds the dis-ease though it is
not real - truthfully we are what you
see out the window on a moonlit night
when it's quiet, when you're timeless,
when you believe believe believe

from the ocean we take you,
covered in seaweed,
the first spark of air
unveils and unbreathes

-November 4, 2016

though we are here,
we will align with the there
it is a tepid bath that we surround ourselves with
some dream we are brave enough to dream

and I will walk about
with this imperceivable shell
my aura, whispering oracular
pleasantries in my ear

she says: you will become that which you will be

and I believe her, I believe

(i am but a seed)

whose colors, when watered, will fall out and bleed

BLOOD BODY

Prayer and Imagination

the gifts bestowed upon me
that reap

more and more gifts

the only tools I'll need,
witch's hands, witch's feet

the others, obsolete,
we are,
the witch's mind

and its dance. dazzling-
the horses, where do they go,
but under the
ocean

and where do I go,
but into a solid earth
home

(receptivity, get in front of me. my hands, they have grown large)

-November 5, 2016

CROWLEY

falling through leaves, thinking on
egyptian eyes,
the fireplace,
santeria
and would the big ones grab my arms,
would they kiss me - they tickled my ankles
in church pews and angels knew my name,
do they see me now? remembering? a
marionette of a woman, looking for the
one pulling the strings, counting the things
that look a bit like clues, rosemary weeping,
cloven shoes

and the red-lit room,

deities, you know me, please,

I am religious,
bound back,
to the pews

BLOOD BODY

we entered the temple to find the good scripture,
our revelation, dictated by an angel with the help
of a daemon, sitting on her shoulder, writing her
rhymes, whispering evils, pouring out wine-

(the moon is divine) like a saint or a serpent
we read the first line, unknowing the flowering
of each word in time, I saw the soot-stained
fingers pointing to the signs, I saw my woman
in black under flickering lamplight

carrying a parcel under cape, dress, and hood
a sacred surrender to that ancient dark book
in search of his parlor in each window she looked,
wandering deftly in alleys and night wood

and she opens his door, her coat falls to the floor
delivering that book - Whore! Whore! Whore!

surrender no more, cherished one, child, the tide
has come in, and you are on fire

...

Babalon, you birthed me,
I am yours yours yours

CROWLEY

I said it felt Light -

don't you see? we are an empty house, waiting to be furnished

-November 6, 2016

BLOOD BODY

if I asked for red nails would you give them to me?
if I dove in the water would you be there to greet me?
if I found you at night would you be there in the morning,
I'm practicing patience but I find it quite boring

because you're not in the air, are you
you're the lining of my skin

the men tried to invoke you
but I'm already in

as a girl I swam in a pool filled with leaves
and dreamt of growing up to be poison ivy

my red hair surrounds you, and you, you do not breathe,
we're choking on the water, and the blood we cannot see

-November 7, 2016

CROWLEY

we drank of The Water -
and said unto thee, three women I see,
my chosen family, ascending in sleep,
and the womb of creativity, who was
that tailed woman, facing away from me
to show me her plenty, to claw at my feet,
who was it but me,

whose image will beckon from
mirrors and phantasy

saying: Do you remember,
our shared history?

-November 8, 2016

Part III

CROWLEY

the curator and his shadowed estate,
what lives in the walls won't come here today
no one is home so he unlocks the white door,
and finds in this room what he's been looking for

see monsters don't live in dripping dark caves
but in the collections of men ensorcelled by the old ways
as if in this rare butterfly he could find his true soul -
the dripping dark caves won't frighten anymore

but madness prefers
the four of these walls
and when the door locks
he is alone with his thoughts

A letter signed in an ink too red:
"Father, forgive me. I thought I could trust them. I didn't mean to let it in."

BLOOD BODY

he wrote me a letter and spoke of his return -
Oh Mother, should I believe him, it's been twenty days,
and see how his handwriting shakes,
oh see, the marks on the page

Oh Mother, I don't believe him. He's been lost in that room,
I know this. The spirits disrupt my sleep at night, and I fear
what they speak, a pact with the devil they said, the man at
the crossroads, and I see him, too, I awoke at midnight with
his hands at my throat. I see him. He spoke-

With his mouth at my ear he told me a tale
of how I would grow thinner and my face
would grow pale, I saw myself descending
down stairs, in a castle unheard of, in the
mists of his lair

Oh, Mother
I think I've grown weak

His story aroused me until I
felt his sharp teeth

CROWLEY

I fell through the hole
and was left with the purple,
the black, and the cold,

I saw the river of Styx
and my friends from the home
I saw my beginning
and the secrets of old,

I stole
a glance at the light
that is wrapped in the dark,

I'm left with
the nothing,
the void
and a
heart

(and I found that enough,
freedom lies in the unwrit
word)

BLOOD BODY

and I see
the gold in the leaves,
the coins in the thicket,
and I'll sleep with their scent,
cedarwood and chocolate

the deeper I sleep,
the more the dream
seeps into waking life,
secret

-November 8, 2016

CROWLEY

I awoke in the reddened sea,
unsure of who had reddened it
the snakes crossed my shoulders
and I am feeling, watercolored

the shackles were a dream
and the fury was no fate,
illusions can test us, and
we can taste them

I am made of too much blood

in the water's reflection,
a girl with two horns

I sink in black sand,
I raise one trembling hand

-November 9, 2016

BLOOD BODY

an arm here, a leg there,
I am dragging myself to completion,
as the hands of the floor below me
try to warm my back,

I am possibly pregnant with
a love-filled sac,

looking for knives,
but courting surrender

happiness is tender,
we will wait one more day

CROWLEY

The sky stayed blue,
as it does when we're morphing,
who is the alchemist above me,
pretending to be Midas, and
who is the shadow
falling into ash

when we let go we relax,
the reptilian woman, unzipping her skin

(oh remember how we cried, staring
up at starlit sky, I remember my home,
an empty throne, realer than these bones)

                                        -November 10, 2016

BLOOD BODY

are we a spiritless corpse reaching out,
or the golden box, wrapped in our fingers

am I red hair, I am

the voice stays the same - am I that?

We mustn't be cut in half

One well - and the fish swimming within

The woman, climbing the walls

Saying: I am skin, I am skin

CROWLEY

someone locked my soul in the red room,

I sit outside and cry, eyes in my hands
I don't see the hand holding out the key

I don't see, I don't see

if we leave the jasmine perfume behind
and if we forget our silks,

we are a body,
we are a body

BLOOD BODY

I love my scales but
mostly in the dark,

just as dreams win our forgiveness,
what comes when we sleep is but
an excused leak,

and we know little of the blackened land,
its charcoal surrender to the shadows of man,
we know nothing of our origins,

the starless night

what monsters creep, what secrets do we keep,
knowing to tell them would be to lie

there are things the Sun doesn't see

-November 11, 2016

CROWLEY

I bought a purple journal, silvered, mooned,
if I lay under the moon will they come get me?

I'm burning too bright, I'll drown in the waters,
melting off the ash

and like an eel find my cove,
I am starlit and old,

wearied by the hours

Mary, maiden
claw-child, bird

destruction pulls at our dress,
we are looking for a new nude

BLOOD BODY

the body won't lie
as it takes the wood from my shoulders
and guides me to the shrine

sit, sit, you seem to deny
the throat's heart beating, bled

lie, lie, and feel the lions at your feet
and cry, weep for every amnesiatic year

you can choose one: cuffs or crown

we are the woman unsure of her throne

CROWLEY

won't a hand cover my mouth so I
can become the evening star,

I will enter the unlit temple
breathing and becoming the unnamed fumes

I was a priestess then,

a lightening rod

Pythoness, let us know god

Pythia, show us the light in the flesh

(satanic succubus,
you know holiness)

-November 12, 2016

BLOOD BODY

locking herself in the drawing room she
Plucked apart, strings and strings,
rational things, afraid of the whisperings
coming from her skirts, what's beneath,
what's below, but a surly and solid moan

and time turned,
as the fires began to consume
and she stood in the middle
of that fanciful room

given to the fire between her legs,
a woman possessed

by every shred of truth that came to earth,

every life,
every urn

the woman of fire
the woman of smoke

-November 13, 2016

a lost language: darling, I'm here

darling, I'm with you

darling, let us be

-November 14, 2016

BLOOD BODY

the woman made of glass -
a mirror, the woman gazing,
glass eyes, glass heart, made of
shards, crystalled over

the woman with her pain on her sleeve

a fog made of rain -

we hid it away so let us be seen -

every moment, every past, welded you to me

CROWLEY

through chapel doors the procession moved,
something inside us is smelling of doom,
and we ran to the dark night, as we always do
playing the piano down below, in Hades' rooms

and what did they tell me?
It's only because it's not true

we would vanish in the night
we would start anew,

if the tortures we were telling
weighed heavier than what we knew

let me sift the gold from the sand -
tell me, tell me, there is another land

woman, woman, woman of the dew

BLOOD BODY

there is no poem for this,
for upside mirrors, the first time
we saw ourselves. and pleasure, and
hope, and consolation, and furor, and
the red dipped in water, and the woman
almost told, and the moment that it came
to us, and the silence that was old. it all flits
away - I'm awakening today

pack your bags - we can't hardly stay

CROWLEY

a new way to see:

we must stretch the measuring tape of healing time a little farther
this is no puzzle, this is no game

this is sitting with, and loving, my pain

and tending that orange flame - we have everything to gain

(there is a room big enough for this, I say)

BLOOD BODY

('like I'm all soul')

a planet with no land, only water

and I became friends with the swimming,

and dream of a dry shore, where you wait for me

-November 15, 2016

Part IV

BLOOD BODY

We Are The Divine Flame

nothing more, nothing more,
but the pools of water that clothe our feet,
bring relief, sharpen our teeth yes a prehistoric
sea creature wagging its tail. god's light, god's ember
we're fools to remember, the red bled out and we were
torn asunder, beating and bleeding and perfectly rendered -

the lovers, taken by the waves, by the curse we are saved,
and by candlelight we prayed, they promised us sinners but
my debts have been paid, and now I'm a body but a flame, a
beloved with no name,

the rose that you remember,
the trembling with no pain

red, only, scarlet
with no shame

-November 18, 2016

CROWLEY

after I had cried, I
saw a woman in the marble,
and how she held to her lover,
despite the skulls of her mind,

I saw a ship capsized,
and the seaman closing their eyes,
I saw the drowning, never asked for,
what had fallen, but the world herself

and that sweet reality,
oh why is the imagination
a festering sea?

BLOOD BODY

They pushed me to the earth and said:
You will be made of fire

CROWLEY

I went looking for a body and found only
two goldfish in a bowl,

it's cold today and so the lizards went away,

the red and green plant, it stretches towards my lamp. is that light enough?

an identity crisis, not the first of its kind, I'm waiting for the ground to crack in two
so I can see what lays beneath. an underworld religion. truth like an oil-slick

we are the woman pulling back skin, will we feel horror or relief?

an open wound - every night some shrew pokes its nose in and cleans me out

an open heart, wide enough for the funeral procession to exit, wide enough for you

I dreamt we wore brown and bled into a couch, I dreamt we wore red

I dreamt of six snakes, each one a necklace, paired with a dress

I dreamt I slept for twenty-five hours, I dreamt that I slept

-November 20, 2016

BLOOD BODY

(the inhalation before, what comes next is shrouded and unformed)
and God may surprise us with presents galore, and we will be smiling,
saying, we should've asked for more

I go to sleep with open palms,

and sleep answers, You must divorce yourself from your thoughts

-November 22, 2016

the woman looking back - and facing forward, her jewel-toned gaze,
flesh imbued, flesh erased, some unity we're craving, some unity we'll taste,
I saw myself in vintage movies and in words from the thirties, in pearls, in
descending, and I was the woman of glow, and there are parts of me I do not
know, but would like to meet. far away from yellow leaves we are the tv set late
at night, two women, unnamed, the water from the well. I am circular, circling
back, finding some meaning in phantasmic fact

always in red, to show what's inside, to show we're not dead

-November 23, 2016

BLOOD BODY

these are songs unsung,
and by the clove tree I'm hung,
dazzled by a ground with a deepening hum,
makes its bed for me, paints me dumb,
paints me red, I swore I'd come, but

when I arrived I only knew numb,
and I fled for awhile to a tower in Babylon,
but I missed the lake, I missed your voice
I was a nocturnal creature, burnt by the sun

-November 24, 2016

critical of the world
critical of my mind
analysis makes me suffer
analysis isn't kind

BLOOD BODY

Perhaps the body is a landing pad,
a makeshift commune, my hands are in the air,
or elsewhere, every night

and at most other times, I was sent by the others,
and so I keep my ear to the wall

the woman apologizing for crying,

such a small thing,
these hands, nail beds,
and this heart, overflows
the river rushing onward,
never apologizing for its
waters

                                        -November 25, 2016

BLOOD BODY

I Forgive - and the box opens and
one small bat flies out - and my
past begins to feel flat, an
empty icebox that
I throw out

nothing but these bones,
saying, we are much older than this
and what happens today is a bright light,
bending forward

(Believe, go to sleep, melt into one)

-November 26, 2016

the reality principle, a life embodied, lay on top of me, I want to be limbs, hips, face - something chosen, prearranged. auburn hair, the only stare, fill my shoes with stones just to walk on land. I saw, in a moment, the hovering craft, from the heart to the crown, and up in the air. I would like to come down now, please, just tell me if that's allowed, please.

if I taste the words (blood, burn, soil) and call it a spell... the sugar is sweet and so we can't tell, what is dream and what is becoming, what is the opposite of a phantom limb?

I wake up heavy, I wake up in light. Let heaven storm earth,
Let this breathing be mine.

BLOOD BODY

Pagan or Christian,
my heart has a mission,
and we will drink wine, either
way.

There is a wisdom that's
quiet, the voice of three
giants, pointing me your
way.

And womanly desire
is my one and only fire,
so I burn myself down,
it's the one and only
way.

'I guess I let love stab me in the chest' but

I am the one holding the dagger

I am the one holding the dagger

I am the one holding the dagger

every time.

BLOOD BODY

Mother Nyx holds my arms as the sun rises behind grey clouds, Child, child, star - you unspool yourself in the primeval evening, you are an angel, angel of the night. As if I made a contract with the otherworld, the ether whirl, I don't awaken at first light. My second home, past the sanctuary, into the sea, the stars, some of our feet rarely meet, split between two worlds. This earth is full of beds, places where we peak, back into our beginnings.

sing me awake, life is a dream of its own, and I remain lucid.

-November 27, 2016

A mist of a woman - I try to pin myself down as I
lay heavily on this bed, the inertia before what? we
were given simple directions, and yet we still feign
complexity, a chest with twenty drawers. we are a
wide island, ruled by one queen, a spider monkey,
thinking of fruit. not thinking at all, just tasting,
seeing, the shores of one world.

I've been in
one casket of solitude, submerged in the sea

thinking without tasting, 'how we move so easily'

BLOOD BODY

I am a
flower playing sudoku, a merciless wand

I begged to start over,
a quiet woman I'll become

(in cashmere, in deep thought,
I woke up one morning and
forgot what I'm not)

-November 28, 2016

My body became a wide and wood-carved canoe,
And for once I laid down in it,
for once I got in.

BLOOD BODY

methods of madness, how to come closer, open the door of that
hand-carved cage, there is a demon of free of expression, the
dream and its lack of walls, there is the one who excuses, and
another that covers the eyes. I am reaching for and removing
the hand that disguises. consciousness, you bruise me. I will
erase all the lines. and drip a little ink for the demon to drink,
it likes these poems. they are: black coves, white sea.

I will bathe in charcoal and make my body an offering, dripping
with a sweat that is mine - there is a home here, half-lived in,
an unheard language, we'd like to learn.

The Magic of Love, The Magic of Woman

A shrine we pass by every day, never asking who it's for.

An innovation, my revelation.

Wondering where we went for all these years.

A coffin, and our honeymoon night.

You brought me to Earth and I brought you to life.

-November 29, 2016

BLOOD BODY

black lipstick and baklava,
in the mirror I looked like a young Arachne,
bent legs, black hair

pleasured sleep, the woman who feeds,
herself and a village

weaving my web, I have mastered all design.

I choose a pattern most beautiful, a pattern that's mine.

-December 1, 2016

what could
get me off my feet but
womanly rage, what could
set my desires aflame, if only
I had one taste - saltwater and
volcanic rock, I felt the earth
moving, and saw the lava
encased in the mountain of a
woman, put in her place, the
comfort of quiet, the safe but
dead weight

BLOOD BODY

cut my dresses in two, and light a velvet plum candle,
scratched on ancient papyri: a list of all my desires
a woman under her own spell. the woman at the helm.

nine wands, and only two choices, fear or faith

let us bathe in the waters of true delight,
there is a secret in the water that I will find

two bands, our hands, and every rose

a secret undulation, black jaguar body, a serpent of a woman there are secrets untold, my own soul, the ocean I bathe in, every ancient woman I have been, watching. waiting, seeing. putting the pen in my hand, the idea in my mind. a chain, an unbreakable chain. the women of mars. the women in me. the elixir - blood-worshipers, moon women, a vampyress, a heretic.

    The Story of a Girl Bitten Into.

-December 2, 2016

BLOOD BODY

There is only this: the conjuring of that sticky warm honey, our own birth into being, there was something I projected out, an hourglass figure, a flower without thorns. There was a dream that I heard, and only later spoke, I promised myself one taste. I promised myself endless faith. A surrender to my favorite card - we would not wait to pick it, blindly. Divination gave way to creation, we already know what we want. And what we are:

a woman marked.

CROWLEY

To deserve what one wants -

We always do, we always will,
I follow my will, into the divine flame,
and cast away those burdens, illusions,
they are not mine. A heavenly design
lays beneath my feet. And I smell it,
I dream it, I let it be.

Standing on the shore, of a calm sea
I let that which I desire
come to me.

-December 3, 2016

BLOOD BODY

Dark Red and Dripping - my desire thickening, tears leave the body like forbidden ghosts, cleansed of something we've already forgot. And I am the priestess, under the moon, remembering her shadow, the woman in blue. We went into battle and came out saved - against white walls I saw the spirits, opening guarded doors. And I awoke one night with my own lore, I am a mystery tradition, all my own. We settle in the dirt and begin to create, I danced in the mirror and for once saw my face. And went to bed bleeding: 'I weave my own fate.'

I swam as an Artist, engulfed by the waves.

CROWLEY

She lays down in an incensed temple,
chapel of her belonging. And every longing,
permeates. An opium den, velvet, demur, the
soft singing of the seventies, her sepia dream.

Robed in the night's beauty, her joy, there are
things living in shadowy corners, creatures,
beasts - blessings that creep. Ideas, dreams,
one potent fantasy, she was the creator, rouging
her lips. A trunk filled with treasures, an attic
filled with light - waltzing to the sounds of a
gramophone, the kind of music that makes you
light a candle.

Splendor, night valley. Olibanum, femininity.

-December 4, 2016

BLOOD BODY

The Grand Desire, fanning the flame
a loosening surrender, I know my own game
butterscotch memory, there is a being who knows
and who teaches, and we recollect, this notion, of
wanting and faith. The woman wanting - the last
one to become. I was a rose amongst gold, knowing
a Duet would be won. Every path up the mountain
led me to you, and to Love, and to the woman I'll be.

There is a child up there, this I do see. I sit back and sip
cold chamomile tea.

Red tinged blue, heart made of goo,
midnight waves encircling, saving,
'smart of the heart' wise and unglued
and stable, my memory line broken,
enslaved by this notion, there is still
something to give up, some wall, a
fortress we built, 'just in case'

Let the drawbridge down, lone girl.
There is safety on both sides.

BLOOD BODY

and how does a young girl get attention?
she sings, or she's taken.

Every fear wishes for its own end -
they do not want to live in an unwelcome home.

The second they leave here, they are no longer known.

BLOOD BODY

I've always needed many names,
many wings, secret things, what's more honest,
the story or the myth? Because I am a mythic woman,
a mystic, a heathen, fallen from heaven, sap from a tree.
And will they name a constellation after me, if I go all the
way, the distance devours until trueness remains.
I fell through the cracks and found my own floor,
in this room I feel holy, the whole of me enflamed.
And each book tells my story, until I'm full of empathy,
for one loving soul. The woman in the woods, the nymph
with wide eyes, and her fleshed form. The woman by the
window, praying, but what for?

-December 5, 2016

Part V

BLOOD BODY

Things that I know:

My heart is a ribbon that I cut into two, I decided what wasn't and I decided on you.

I stood in a graveyard and called it a home, since I was a child I have felt old.

I once treated a girl how men treated me, I lived out a pattern that I could not see.

Our bodies are made of clay, you taught me what it feels like when someone will stay.

I've had this name for my whole life, and I don't know why but it's never felt right.

-December 6, 2016

I want to write something that you'll understand-
my words were once cloaks that I kept myself in.
an illusionist, gesticulating on stage, and the woman
cut in half, with a smile on her face.

When I talk about flowers I'm talking about me-
and a place I call home when I talk of the sea.
and when I talk about dew you'll know what I mean,
for once I'll be fogless, for once I'll be seen.

Transparent, tangible, my heart on my sleeve.

BLOOD BODY

woman's desire as hubris,

her entity, obscenity
an exhibitionist, existing

her kindness, cause for cruelty
her masochism, her masochism, her masochism

in a dream she sang: "I want to be objectified"

If you see it, then I'll see it, too
If you feel it, then I'll feel it, too

man-killer, succubus,
the woman who snapped
two footprints on her back

blood-thirsty vengeance,
mutiny, we've lost you

rage, we've lost you

anger, we've lost you

pain, we touch your walls
in a darkened room,

secretly,
quietly

or not at all

(Rome was the first to fall)

BLOOD BODY

every woman was a woman but me, you see
and I was the final girl, with blood on her teeth

only violence and terror could sanctify me

until I found pleasure, my delayed puberty

CROWLEY

I soaked in a tub and
pulled off my skin, I was
rosy and panting, hot and sanguine
Alive! and a womanly shriek, the bowels
of hell, spoke through me. No longer the
days of my intruder dreams, where I opened
my mouth but just couldn't scream. The hysteric,
crying but submitting to the strong orderlies.

Abject horror, what's underneath-
blood boiled, devil's tail, two unheard of wings

the mouth sings, the cunt bleeds, I want to be Seen.

-December 7, 2016

CREATRIX

unbridled and white,
torn dress, taupe leather restraints,
unbuckled. unbecoming, fugitive -
failed fumigation, the heart lives on,
an injured fox, we survived muteness,
we were fightless, we went mad but
never got mad, we were faithful.

Creatrix, your body unwove itself and a part of me cried.

I was a ghost at fifteen and a woman at five.

-December 8, 2016

Spider Witch,

rouges her lips, and writes her own fate
I felt you in shadows, I called out your name
I blackened my hair, I caught you live prey,
I shape-shift at night and four become eight,
I fell into slumber, you devoured my face

(what's left but womanly grace?)

BLOOD BODY

Whittle me down until I am only core,
the blankets I curl beneath, I know what they're for.
But deep in the night we will open the door,
the demon must feed, sow seeds, and explore

Candlewick, girl,
we follow the heart and begin to unfurl,
honest desire, you'll become my anchor,
a string tied from my womb to the floor

I am fervent, perverted,
- I am yours

CROWLEY

I try to imagine a twin,

1. she is smaller than me, smaller hands,
smaller feet, smaller teeth. white flour
hair, imploring, 'forgive... forgive... be
free...'

a white sun blanches any and all original sin,

2. she is meaner than me, sharper, redder,
blacker, paler, demanding, controlling, she
grabs my hands 'there, it is done, was that
so hard?' she does not care.

a snake sees all things but has no empathy,

3. she is louder than me, her cries are louder,
more real, more honest, it all begins and ends
with this crying. she is teenaged, she cries and
so she is free. my own brown-haired Lethe.

a bright-eyed soul is not cursed with memory,

I try to imagine a twin, and she looks like a saint-
she looks like me.

there is a holiness around her that only death brings.

-December 10, 2016

BLOOD BODY

I become transparent
and I camouflage,

I wisp into nothing,
a story ends at present day,

we throw the pages into water,
mush. bled ink. fish food. nothing.

Clarity, look right through me,
I am only my dreams.

Not the unconscious dance,
but the conjurer's steady chant

Not the water,
but the castles on the shore

Oh Poltergeist,
I am a demon-bride,

whose flowers are purple and dry,
whose story is uneternal, infernal,
and whose mouth quivers for blood,

demon-child, you burst into flames
between the pews of this church,
you snarl and you cry and heaven
lets you die,

you are ashes on the floor;
exorcism. evil falls asleep in the
soft bed of nihility

BLOOD BODY

The Walking Weaver

I am not afraid of death, I crave new life,
I bare my fangs for it, I salivate, I am
filled with the images I want to create -
I tore up my horoscope and forgot about fate.

The Priestess Surrenders

I slice my small finger with the sharp of a thorn,
I am ready for a pact, I am ready to be reborn,
the moon doesn't know me, she introduces herself,
I make up a name, she's never heard it before.

A Woman knows Hell,
she's been there before.

It is not she-demons,
it is not Lilith,
it is not unseen ghosts,
opening kitchen drawers,

no, that is her,

It is not the devouring woman,
asking for more…

It is the neurosis, her anxiety,
jealousy, the fears she cannot speak,
and abandonment, how it curls at her feet,

It is the madness, an inch from her eyes,
crouching, always, that violent beast.

Self-destruction, self-destruction,
I once wished I had no emotions.

I went to the doctor, he made me a concoction,
A Woman knows Hell, and she goes there often.

-December 11, 2016

BLOOD BODY

Echidna,

Mother of All Monsters,
I kiss you, and know you well,
I, too, came out crawling and
slithering, with glancing black
eyes, and I, too, found a cave,
in which I could lie.

Snake-woman, you have my heart,
and your face looks like mine.

We are the progenitors of horrors,
those that guard golden apples,
and tell riddles to kings.

-December 12, 2016

I was crawling through an underground tunnel when:
there was no more air, or there was too much air, old air,
stale air, recirculating, thoughts I had thought before but
brought no feeling. Only pleasure pulled me through, my
lavender salve, my sweet invite back into a body, back into
a being ripped away, why does woman live dually, the eye
always watching, and the woman watched.

Analysis is a sharp knife,
and this operating table, an anxious self-abnegation.
We follow the spool of thread or the slicing of skin back to a
childhood's past, and there we sit: sicker, choking on answers
we've learned to rehearse. What left these scars? the injury or
the autopsy? the transgression or the dissection? the memory or
the remembering?

Who ripped the skin off? saying, let us begin again, darling...

oh, and let us forget.

BLOOD BODY

Sibylline, how many eyes do you have, and
how you'd like to pluck them out. Silvered
slivers, the moon made me whole, slender
but curved. I offered two hands and some
red rope, to be bound is to hope- the first
line in a bible found underground. We are
moles, masquerading as medicine women.
Digging holes in the lining of our skin.....

They found me covered in crescents - little
indents, from the nails of many women.
Each hand grabbed at my limbs, before
falling into the ocean. Lunacy's last
gasp, her analgesic poison.

-December 13, 2016

River-women,
those that jump from high cliffs.

Lake-dwellers, who come face to face
with a chosen fate, stones tethered to
frail and unforgiving waists.

Naiads, ancestors, foremothers, friends,
women whose death came long before their end.

To the water they return, washed of all their sin,
the marks of hands not belonging to them.

BLOOD BODY

Some live in the darkest of blues, and she did, oh how she hid, like an animal. In the cover of night, she shape-shifts and flies, a bat when she's sad, or a wolf when she's mad, and every sound she makes is left unheard, falling in the forest and never quite known.

The stars keep her secrets, they do not pass judgement on women or beasts. And in the morning before the mirror, she washes away blood instead of dried tears. And she will return later that night, to the forest of fears. She's been doing this for a thousand years.

-December 14, 2016

The Salacious Woman
pink-tongued and grabbing,
burnt by a cross that predicted her ending,
she would share her throne with a young girl,
the innocent virgin, until the girl grew up to be
A Salacious Woman.

BLOOD BODY

Could I let myself feel safe?

I'd like to feel safe.

I was on an island, for once,
and dreamt of floods every night.

I kept my boat nearby, out of the
corner of my eye, at all times.

I hallucinated rain clouds,
I packed up my things.

I was on an island, for once,
but I dreamt of floods every night.

Like a sorceress, or a prophet,
we opened the locket, to remember what things
call out our names. And with pupils quite large, we
whispered our charms, and pressed the promise to our
slow beating hearts.

There's a field where I will lay, there's the imagining of it
today. There's the hope in between, which lights up the way.
(I make my own fate, I make my own fate. I write down these
words and proclaim my faith.)

BLOOD BODY

We are not afraid of that which we find beautiful,
I cover words in silks and they turn into miracles,
escape routes hidden behind the turn of a phrase,
I woke to find no reason for this self-afflicted pain,

Anxieties are like ghosts, they live off of fear
I stopped being afraid, and they simply disappeared.

-December 15, 2016

The devil's plaything,
he raises her up, and she laughs lightly
as she levitates, "It feels like a warm bath."
or like becoming a butterfly. They play these
games on foggy days, when the sun has gone
missing and is replaced by a lavender glow. On
clear nights when the moon shines through the
curtains, she goes catatonic. She is stiff limbs and
an unmoving face. Placeholders. The nurses know
she's been claimed.

The priests pass by her door, they under strict orders:
Do not get between the devil and his plaything.

BLOOD BODY

A warrior woman whispered in my ear, her language
cutting, it cut me up. Illusions that floated about in the sky,
and from the mouths of many women, women with scars, we
see them, and we know, and together we dug a row of graves,
saying, see what you've done. To no one in particular, to everyone,
to people we'd never see again. I no longer want to be buried.

But I do not know how to live.

I was once a holder of the red poison, I was once
a vampire in the night, I was once furious. I was once
lethal.

I lived like a dead woman. A mouth full of vengeance.

And oh how I danced, I danced, I danced.

Alive, with blackened eyes.

Stab wounds bleeding out on the subway.

Hellish fiend, nocturnal demon.

-December 16, 2016

CROWLEY

The demonic urges of the earth,
nature knows my veins, it sleeps in me,
erupts in dreams, stares back at me in the
mirror, I'm surprised by my eyes, those of a
hungering tree.

Whose sap is bright red, and who begs to be cut down.
Destruction, baby, cut me clean.

I smell your aggression, and I'll let you be mean.
And with a sigh of relief, I'll return to our sea.
Driftwood, satiated by a lover's chokehold,
and then his embrace.

BLOOD BODY

The blood remembers,
and so do I, ripped tights,
whiskey, glorious burning,
I was a fire no one could stop,
a girl glowing with radiation,
lighting up in the east village.

I was a kitten with claws.

Lust has been the thick tail dragging behind me,
black and scaly, since the dawn of time. Once small,
and then big, gargantuan, that of a behemoth. I cut it
off once, but it grew back.

I let it curl around me, my body's sweet infinity,
serpentine and slithering. Thicker than
both my legs put together.

-December 17, 2016

BLOOD BODY

We never trusted innocence,
and so it became an island far away,
the place where my body had lain.

-December 18, 2016

Part VI

BLOOD BODY

I fell asleep in the woods,
an omen,
I fell asleep in the woods,
open,

I fell asleep in the woods,
a woman,
a woman,
a woman.

-

I ran through the darkness, after one butterfly. Whose wings called me crazy, and who witnessed my cries. It said: you are not a tree, rooted, unmoving. You have wings like me, you psychotic woman.

Saint, witch, or psycho?
Saint, witch, or psycho?

-December 19, 2016

I awoke in a coffin
my eyes shot open,
and I sucked in air,
buried in white, but
feeling quite black,
I sat near my death,
and made the sign
of the cross. I am an
angel or demon, no
one would tell me which,
but they whisper about me,
so I know something's strange.
And curses fall from my mouth,
and I say 'oh I'm sorry, sorry,' repenting
my sin. I am chained at the ankles, but
the rust sets me free, I am too old for
the memories that used to plague me.
I push at the lid but the light hurts my
eyes, I fall back asleep until the arrival of
night. And then I crawl out, see a cemetery,
and sigh. I'm beginning again, a stab at a life.
I wield my knife well, I know how to fight. I
sleepwalk for awhile, following the scent of
fire, and happen upon a Bacchanalia, the first
of its kind. Ecstasy, oh ecstasy, you know me
quite well. Each life found us sweating, and
panting into each other. I will burn for you.
I will burn for you. I will burn it all down.

BLOOD BODY

Volcano woman...
I see your flood. You do not hide that which is inside,
you are a hell unto yourself. And I will bathe in you
and burn it all off, skin which is not mine, a face that
does lie. I will be resurrected, and enjoy in this, the melting.
Bones bones bones, it seems they are made of metal,
something that withstands. I lay back and relax as the
blacksmith welds me back to life. I am a funeral, today.
A winter solstice who knows how to say:

each bat that flies through your open window
blesses the forehead of a child. You are a trick,
an alien witch. You are the dawning of new light
and the demons dancing under a sun that destroys,
they do not mind death, they scheme and they devise
how to once again die, the cradle of life kisses, and they
have more than nine lives. Oh, eustress, you've led me to
here. I will not deny that I get off on fear. I'm glad to find
my own kind - the creatures and spirits. The vampires and
wives.

-December 21, 2016

A woman creates.
She cups the dirt from her grave -
something new she will make.

A woman hides.
Some plan(t)s grow better without the light -
they prefer to be seen by only her eyes.

A woman dissolves.
As the moon wanes, she peels her clothes off -
she returns to the water, it's her light, she's the moth.

A woman knows.
There's a voice in her body whose wisdom is old -
it tells her what to do, and she does what she's told.

BLOOD BODY

I woke up with no scars.
Fresh skin.

I pointed to my memories and tried to tell their stories,
but something hushed me and said:

"There is a place where none of this happened.
Remember.
Remember to forget."

-December 26, 2016

CROWLEY

I bathe in my own blood and I drink it
I drink it I drink it I drink,

I'm swallowing every last warm drop of me.

Until I'm as red as a rose - a tenderly thing.

BLOOD BODY

I'm good at cutting off my own limbs.

Keep your knife at your side, I'll use mine.
I'll use mine.
I'll use mine.

-December 27, 2016

Rest easy, small creature.

You are on dry land,
after drowning.

-December 28, 2016

BLOOD BODY

Listless and sleeping,
my tender heart weeping,
each tear holding a new life,
handing it back, and abandoning,
thank you thank you thank you
for emptying me out. slumber,
I move under the beast as it
sleeps, a floating figure. I'm
waiting for the end of gut-
drenched December.

(in the heart of winter I've been warmed by your embers,
this I will remember, a love so tender, it tenderized me)

-December 30, 2016

A Waterless Body

I prayed for a waterless body,
for lungs, not gills. Let me evolve,
a little, let me walk on land. I am a
deep-sea diver praying for sand. You
wait by the shore, and from the ocean
I rise. I've been praying for you for my
whole life. There is a home on the shore,
and part of it's mine. I love you, I breathe
you, we're the earth, we're the sky.

-January 1, 2017

BLOOD BODY

I try to imagine a twin,

she is Safe. she is Here.

She speaks of her surrenders like a translucent deer.

She is steady, she is knowing.

Two eyes full of sadness that soon disappears.

A portal, a clearing. A crop circle, a feeling.

I try to imagine a twin,

and she's no longer there.

She crawled into my bones and tangled herself in my hair.

-January 2, 2017

Fear was a cloak,

fear was a skin.

Fear was a poison that I

soaked myself in.

Spell:

Exsanguination, transfusion.
Exsanguination, transfusion.
Exsanguination, transfusion.

-January 6, 2016, Blood Body

www.ingramcontent.com/pod-product-compliance
Lightning Source LLC
LaVergne TN
LVHW041623070426
835507LV00008B/425